CENGAGE Learning

Drama for Students, Volume 5

Staff

Editorial: David M. Galens, *Editor*. Christopher Busiel, Clare Cross, John Fiero, David M. Galens, Lane A. Glenn, Carole Hamilton, Elizabeth Judd, Sheri Metzger, Annette Petrusso, Arnold Schmidt, *Entry Writers*. Tim Akers, Brigham Narins, Kathy Wilson, *Contributing Editors*. James Draper, *Managing Editor*. Kathy Wilson, *"For Students" Line Coordinator*. Jeffery Chapman, *Programmer/Analyst*.

Research: Victoria B. Cariappa, *Research Team Manager*. Andy Malonis, Barb McNeil, *Research Specialists*. Tamara C. Nott, Tracie A. Richardson, Corrine A. Stocker, Cheryl L. Warnock, Robert Whaley, *Research Associates*. Patricia T. Ballard, Phyllis P. Blackman, *Research Assistants*.

Permissions: Maria Franklin, *Interim Permissions Manager*. Kimberly F. Smilay, *Permissions*

Specialist. Kelly A. Quin, *Permissions Associate*. Sandra K. Gore, *Permissions Assistant*.

Graphic Services: Randy Bassett, *Image Database Supervisor*. Robert Duncan and Michael Logusz, *Imaging Specialists*. Pamela A. Reed, *Imaging Coordinator*. Gary Leach, *Macintosh Artist*.

Product Design: Cynthia Baldwin, *Product Design Manager*. Cover Design: Michelle DiMercurio, *Art Director*. Page Design: Pamela A. E. Galbreath, *Senior Art Director*.

Copyright Notice

and other applicable laws. The authors and editors of this work have added value to the underlying factual material herein through one or more of the following: unique and original selection, coordination, expression, arrangement, and classification of information. All rights to this publication will be vigorously defended.

This book is printed on acid-free paper that meets the minimum requirements of American National Standard for Information Sciences—Permanence Paper for Printed Library Materials, ANSI Z39.48-1984.

ISBN 0-7876-2754-2
ISSN 1094-9232
Printed in the United States of America

10 9 8 7 6 5 4 3 2

Equus

Peter Shaffer

1973

Introduction

Peter Shaffer was inspired to write *Equus* by the chance remark of a friend at the British Broadcasting Corporation (BBC). The friend recounted to Shaffer a news story about a British youth who blinded twenty-six horses in a stable, seemingly without cause. Shaffer never confirmed the event or discovered more of the details, but the story fascinated him, provoking him "to interpret it in some entirely personal way." His dramatic goal, he wrote in a note to the play, was "to create a mental world in which the deed could be made comprehensible."

Equus depicts the state of mind of Alan Strang, the imaginative, emotionally-troubled stableboy who serves as the play's protagonist. In relating his themes, Shaffer combines psychological realism with expressionistic theatrical techniques, employing such devices as masks, mime, and dance. The ongoing dialogue between Alan and Dr. Martin Dysart, the boy's analyst, illustrates Shaffer's theme of contrary human impulses toward rationality and irrationality. Curing Alan, making the boy socially acceptable and more "normal," Dysart frets, will at the same time squelch an important spark of passionate creativity in the youth.

Equus, which some critics labeled a "psycho-drama," premiered in London at the Old Vic Theatre on July 26, 1973. The production was a huge success, impressing both audiences and critics alike and securing Shaffer's reputation as an important contemporary dramatist. *Equus* had its American premiere at New York's Plymouth Theatre on October 24, 1974, and later received the Antoinette Perry (Tony) Award, the Outer Critics Circle Award, and the New York Drama Critics Circle Award. The play was adapted into a film in 1977.

Author Biography

Peter Shaffer and his twin brother Anthony (also a playwright and novelist) were born May 15, 1926, in Liverpool, England. Peter attended St. Paul's School in London, graduating in 1944, near the end of World War II. For the remainder of the war, he was conscripted to work as a coal miner; because a large number of England's adult male workforce were off fighting the war, many labor positions were filled by women, children, and young adults.

After the war Shaffer attended Trinity College, Cambridge, from which he received a degree in 1950. Following graduation he moved to New York City, where he worked in a book store and the New York Public Library. He returned to London in 1954, working for music publishers Bosey & Hawkes. He began writing scripts for radio and television during this period as well as serving as literary critic for the journal *Truth* from 1956-57.

Shaffer's first stage play, *Five Finger Exercise,* was produced in 1958. He followed it with the paired one-acts *The Private Ear* and *The Public Eye* in 1962. In 1963 Shaffer cowrote, with noted stage director Peter Brook (*Marat/Sade*), the screenplay for Brook's film adaptation of William Golding's novel *Lord of the Flies.*

Shaffer's reputation as an accomplished dramatist was secured by the 1964 premiere of his full-length work *Royal Hunt of the Sun: A Play*

Concerning the Conquest of Peru. The play—which creatively blends ritual, dance, music, and drama—reenacts the sixteenth-century Spanish conquest, by Francisco Pizarro, of the Incan empire. The Incas dominated the culture of western South America in the fifteenth and sixteenth centuries; the center of their empire lay in what is now Peru, a country founded by Pizarro. Shaffer's plays of subsequent years include the one-act *Black Comedy* (1965), a piece based on a device borrowed from Chinese theatre in which actors pretend to be in total darkness although the stage is lit.

Shaffer's 1970 full-length *The Battle ofShrivings* was widely considered a disappointment, but the playwright followed it with *Equus* (1973), a play that is generally considered his greatest achievement to date. *Equus* received the Antoinette Perry (Tony) Award for best play as well as the New York Drama Critics Circle Award. Shaffer also wrote the screenplay for the film adaptation of *Equus* in 1977.

In 1979, Shaffer produced what is generally considered his best-known work, *Amadeus,* which he has described as "a fantasia on events in [18th century composer Wolfgang Amadeus] Mozart's life." Like *Equus, Amadeus* is a probing exploration of the human psyche, centering on the royal court composer Antonio Salieri and his jealousy of Mozart's seemingly effortless brilliance. Mozart is portrayed as a vulgar, self-centered genius, a sort of prototypical rock star. The play won the 1980 Tony award, and the 1984 film adaptation won Academy

Awards for best picture and best screenplay adaptation (for Shaffer's script). Shaffer's plays since *Amadeus* include *Yonadab: The Watcher* (1985) and the popular comedy *Lettice andLovage* (1987).

With a long-standing reputation for craftsmanship, Shaffer's career is marked by theatrical success and prestigious honors. In addition to his many popular successes in drama, he is a fellow of the Royal Society of Literature, a member of the Dramatists Guild, and was granted the title Commander of the British Empire in 1987.

Act I

The play opens on two scenes: Alan Strang fondles the head of a horse, who in turn nuzzles the boy's neck; subsequently, Dr. Martin Dysart addresses a lecture audience about the case of Alan Strang, a troubled boy of seventeen who blinded six horses. Dysart begins his narrative with the visit by his friend Hesther Salomon, a magistrate who managed to persuade the court to put Alan in a psychiatric hospital rather than in prison. As the action on the stage enacts this recollection, Salomon tells the doctor that she feels something very special about the boy. Dysart agrees to see Alan, although he is already overworked.

In their first session, Alan is evasive, singing advertising jingles in response to Dysart's questions. Alan is clearly startled when the psychiatrist coolly responds to the jingles as if Alan were speaking normally. Upon conclusion of the meeting, the boy is reluctant to leave the doctor's office, and, as he is finally ushered out, he makes a point of passing "dangerously close" to Dysart.

Returning to the lecture format, Dysart reveals to his audience that he is suffering nightmares in which he is a ancient priest sacrificing children, on whom he sees the face of Alan. At the same time, however, Dysart feels he has achieved a breakthrough with his patient, who is beginning to open up. Dysart pays a visit to Alan's parents in the hopes of learning something of the boy's background. The father, Frank, is still at work, but his wife Dora informs the doctor that Alan was always captivated by horses, particularly a story about a talking horse called Prince, who could only be ridden by one special boy. Alan also memorized a Biblical passage about horses in the Book of Job; he was particularly taken with the Latin word *Equus*. When Frank returns home, he tells the doctor that he blames Alan's problems on the Biblical passages about the death of Jesus, which Dora read to the boy night after night. Frank shares his belief that religion is only so much "bad sex."

Dysart must discover the reason behind Alan's screams of "Ek!" in the night. Although Alan has grown more communicative, he still resists interviewing, making the doctor answer his own queries for each question Dysart poses. Question follows question, but when Dysart asks Alan directly why he cries out at night, the boy reverts to singing television jingles. Dysart dismisses Alan, and this reverse psychology causes Alan to begin talking about his first experience with a horse. At the beach, a man let Alan join him on his horse and ride as fast as the boy liked. Alan's parents saw him, became worried, and caused him to fall. Alan claims this was the last time he ever rode a horse.

In three unexpected visits, Dysart acquires a great deal of new information. From Dora Strang, he learns about a particularly graphic image of

Christ, "loaded down with chains," on his way to crucifixion, which used to hang above Alan's bed. It was torn down by Frank after one of their frequent fights about religion and replaced with a photograph of a horse that pleased Alan immensely. In the second visit, Mr. Dalton, the stable owner, informs Dysart that Alan was introduced to the stables by a young employee of his, Jill Mason. Dalton comments that Alan was always a terrific worker before the blinding incident but that for some time he suspected the boy may have been taking the horses out at night to ride them. Finally, Frank Strang pays Dysart a visit, describing with great difficulty how he once discovered Alan reciting a parody of a Biblical genealogy and then kneeling reverently in front of the photograph of the horse and beating himself with a coat hanger. Frank also reveals that Alan was out with a girl the night he blinded the horses.

In their next conversation, Dysart asks Alan more directly about Jill. The boy calls the doctor "Bloody Nosey Parker!" and in turn asks about Dysart's relationship with his wife, suspecting that the couple never has sex. Startled that Alan so quickly discovered his "area of maximum vulnerability," Dysart orders the boy out of his office. Speaking later with Hesther, Dysart laments his sterile marriage. Hesther reminds Dysart that it is his job to make Alan normal again, but Dysart questions the value of what society views as normal. When Alan next comes before the doctor he is more subdued, and Dysart succeeds in hypnotizing him through a game he calls "Blink." In this state, Alan is persuaded to discuss in detail his ritualistic and ecstatic midnight rides. An expressionistic, theatrical enactment of one of these rides brings the first act to a close.

Act II

In another monologue, Dysart continues to question rhetorically the value of his profession. The speech is interrupted by the entrance of a nurse, who reports that Mrs. Strang has slapped Alan after violently refusing the lunch she brought for him. Dysart confronts Mrs. Strang and orders her to leave. She expresses to the doctor the frustration she feels as a mother, wanting Dysart to understand that what is wrong with Alan is not a result of anything she or Frank did to him. "I only know he was my little Alan," she mourns, "and then the Devil came."

In a subsequent discussion with Dysart, Alan denies anything that he said under hypnosis. At the same time, however, the boy suggests that he would take a "truth drug," to make him reveal things he is withholding.

Talking again with Hesther, Dysart reveals further reluctance to cure Alan, especially if it means denying him the worship which is central to his life. The doctor envies the boy's passion. Alan later apologizes for having denied what he said under hypnosis and acknowledges that he understands why he is in the hospital. Dysart is extremely pleased. Sending for Alan in the middle of the night, he gives the boy a placebo—an aspirin that he tells Alan is a truth drug—and with encouragement Alan begins to speak freely about his relationship with Jill Mason.

Jill started talking to Alan one night after work, commenting how she noticed his beautiful eyes and obvious affection for the horses. She suspected that, like her, Alan found horses, especially their eyes, very sexy. Jill encouraged Alan to go to a pornographic film with her, and in the cinema, seeing a woman naked for the first time, Alan was mesmerized. Suddenly noticing his father in the audience of the film, however, Alan was ashamed to be caught at a "dirty" movie (though he was more shaken to discover his father there). Alan refused to go home with Frank, insisting it was proper to see Jill home first.

On their walk home, Alan made two important discoveries: first, he finally saw his father as man just like any other, and second, he realized he wanted very much to be with Jill, to see her naked and to touch her. Alan eagerly accepted when Jill suggested that they go off together but was disturbed to learn that her destination was the stables. The young couple undressed, but Alan found himself unable to touch Jill, "hearing" the disapproval of Equus. Furious, Alan ordered Jill out of the stables, took up a pick, and put out the eyes of Dalton's horses.

With the repressed pain of Alan's angry and destructive act now brought to the surface, Dysart feels he can relieve the boy of his nightmares and other mental anguish. But Dysart's monologue that ends the play is the strongest indictment yet of the work he is doing. Dysart laments that in treating Alan, he will relieve the boy not only of his pain but of all feeling, inspiration, and imagination. As for himself, the lesson of Alan has showed him how lost he truly is: "There is now, in my mouth, this sharp chain," Dysart concludes. "And it never comes out."

Characters

Harry Dalton

A stable owner. He is bitter about Alan's blinding of his horses and feels the boy should be in prison, not "in a hospital at the tax-payers' expense." Before the blinding incident, however, Dalton was extremely friendly and supportive of Alan when the boy came to work at his stable; he told Alan, "the main rule is: enjoy yourself."

Martin Dysart

A psychiatrist in his mid-forties. He reluctantly accepts Alan as a patient, persuaded by his lawyer friend Hester Salomon that there is something special about the boy. While Dysart is able to help the young man face his problems, the experience of analyzing Alan has a profound effect on Dysart's view of his own life as well. Alan's probing questions about Dysart's relationship with his wife —a Scottish dentist named Margaret—causes the Doctor to reflect upon how estranged they have become as a couple. They have no children and share minimal, if any, sexual intimacy. Dysart regrets how "briskly" he and his wife have lived their lives together.

When he compares himself to the boy he is treating for insanity, Dysart questions himself. He can cure Alan and make the boy more "normal," but he regrets that the cost of this process may be Alan losing his unique passion and creativity. Dysart comes to doubt the value of his own work and, perhaps as a result, suffers nightmares. In these dreams he sees himself as a high priest killing children in ritual sacrifice rather than healing them.

Horseman

The Horseman, who Alan describes as "a college chap," and Frank later calls "upper class riffraff," provides six-year-old Alan his first experience riding a horse. Alan's parents are frightened for Alan's safety, and Frank pulls his son violently from the horse, causing Alan to fall. The Horseman is incredulous at the anger of Alan's parents. He flippantly calls Frank a "stupid fart" and makes a point of starting his horse so that its hooves cover the family with sand and water as he rides away. The same actor who plays the Horseman also plays Nugget, one of Dalton's horses that Alan takes for his midnight rides. This actor is among the chorus of six actors who depict horses.

Jill Mason

In her early twenties, "pretty and middle class." Jill introduced Alan to Harry Dalton, helping the boy get a job in Dalton's stables. Jill is attracted to Alan and encourages him to take her to a pornographic film, where they run into Alan's father. Later, in the stable, Jill and Alan have a failed sexual encounter. In his shame, Alan sends Jill away and blinds the horses, a deed which catalyzes the play's dramatic action. Dalton reports that Jill had a nervous breakdown after hearing of Alan's act.

Hesther Salomon

A magistrate. She brings Alan to Dysart after pleading with the court to allow the boy a psychiatric evaluation. She is a friend to Dysart and hears him out as he relates his personal problems—many of which he has been forced to face as a result of treating Alan. She tries to persuade Dysart that his psychiatric work has value and that curing Alan is an important task: "The boy's in pain, Martin," she observes. "That's all I see. In the end."

Alan Strang

A "lean boy of seventeen," who is arrested after blinding six horses at Harry Dalton's stable where he works. He appears very troubled; in his first session with psychiatrist Martin Dysart, Alan will only respond by singing advertising jingles. Alan has developed a complex ritual of devotion to the god Equus, which he practices through ecstatic midnight rides on Dalton's horses. Alan's pagan ritual transfers much of his mother's Christian faith onto the image of the horse, which Alan associates with the forbidden since the disaster of his first riding experience. Frustrated and ashamed following his sexual failure with Jill, Alan blinds the horses to protect himself from the vengeance of Equus, who "saw" the boy in disgrace.

Media Adaptations

- *Equus* was adapted into a film in 1977 by United Artists and directed by Sidney Lumet. Shaffer's script received an Academy Award nomination for best screenplay based on material from another medium. The film also received Academy Award nominations for best actor (Richard Burton portraying Dr. Dysart) and best supporting actor (Peter Firth as Alan).

- A BBC sound recording of *Equus* was made in 1984 (distributed in the United States by Audio-Forum).

After resisting Dysart's initial attempts to help him, Alan gradually grows more comfortable with the psychiatrist. Although Dysart regrets that curing the boy might give him a life as devoid of real passion as the doctor's own, professional considerations prevail. Alan purges a great deal of pain in his later sessions with Dysart, and the play concludes with the implication that the doctor will continue to heal the boy's mental anguish.

Dora Strang

Alan's mother, a former school teacher (Alan declares proudly to Dysart, "She knows more than you"). She is religious, frequently talking to Alan about the Bible (much to the frustration of her atheist husband, Frank). Dora also feels she married beneath herself socially, a regret that shows itself in various ways. She comes from a "horsey family," while Frank finds riding to be an affectation of "upper class riffraff." She did not want Alan to work in a shop because "shops are common."

Dora visits Alan in the hospital, and when the boy throws his lunch at her, she slaps him. She regret this act of violence but expresses to Dysart the level of her frustration under the present circumstances. She is incredulous that Dysart would view Alan's violence as a product of his upbringing. "I only know he was my little Alan," she mourns, "and then the Devil came."

Frank Strang

Alan's father, a printer by trade. He is a self-declared atheist, which goes hand-in-hand with his political beliefs (Dysart calls him an "old-type Socialist. Relentlessly self-improving"). He frequently quotes Karl Marx's adage, "Religion is the opium of the people" in response to his wife's religious beliefs. As an atheist, he sees religion as "just bad sex," holding his wife responsible for Alan's psychological condition.

Frank comes alone to Dysart's office to describe to the doctor how he once discovered Alan reciting a parody of a Biblical genealogy and then kneeling reverently in front of a photograph of a horse and beating himself with a coat hanger. Frank also reveals to Dysart that Alan was out with a girl the night he blinded the horses, neglecting to mention that he knows this because he encountered the couple in a pornographic cinema.

Themes

Freedom

There is an ethical ambiguity explored in *Equus,* the conflict between two ideas of right. The freedom of the individual to do whatever he or she wants must always be balanced with the social need to limit this freedom when a person's actions are harmful to others. This is certainly the case with Alan's shocking crime; society's highest priority in this case is to put Alan away, or to cure his psychological distress so that, hopefully, he will not again cause such harm. Dysart recognizes that he cannot simply allow Alan to act entirely of his own will, but at the same time he is loathe to administer a cure that will most likely quell or kill the boy's imagination and passion. The doctor also worries that the force driving Alan's actions is something closer to instinct rather than a simple mental problem. He is concerned that squelching such impulses will essentially rob Alan of all identity. Yet the concerns of society as a whole prevail in this case; Alan's actions, if left unchecked, will ultimately hinder the freedom and happiness of others.

God and Religion

Not only is religion a significant theme in *Equus,* it has shown itself important to Shaffer's writing throughout his long career. Shaffer is fascinated by the human need to believe in a god, to discover a suitable form of worship. In this play the primary theological distinction is between Christianity and paganism (in the form of a horse-god). Alan has been brought up in a Christian faith by his mother, but the horrific tales of Christ's crucifixion disturbed him. He creates his own religion, channeling Christian beliefs and practices into his worship of the god Equus, a horse figure that is far more comforting to him than the bloodied Jesus. Dr. Dysart, with his passion for classical culture, makes associations between Alan's beliefs and the ancient, pagan Greek society which is viewed as so influential upon Western civilizations (Greek culture embraced many gods who they believed influenced various facets of their lives; they built a system of arts and social government that is often cited as a model for modern society). Dysart understands intellectually (and begins to feel genuinely) that, as he says, "life is only comprehensible through a thousand local gods."

Growth and Development

Horse figures play an enormous role in Alan's development. Images of the horse pervade the play, appropriate for a near archetypal figure which has such important historical and cultural associations. Dora Strang relates how Alan was fascinated as a boy with a historical fact regarding the conquest of the Americas: when Christian cavalry arrived in the new world, the indigenous people often mistook horse and rider for one creature, a four-legged animal with the powers of a god. This anecdote greatly influences the development of Alan's personal mythology of Equus; as he matures and begins his naked midnight rides, this mythos incorporates sexual elements as well. This is depicted in the last scene of Act One. In a near sexual/religious frenzy, Alan rides the horse, crying, "Bear me away! Make us One Person!"

Other encounters with horse images, or actual horses, were also important to Alan's development —the storybook his mother read to him over and over, the odd photograph of a horse which replaced the portrait of Christ's crucifixion, and the traumatic experience of being pulled from a horse by his father after a thrilling oceanfront ride. Other cultural associations with horses—their speed and power, their majestic carriage—make plausible to a contemporary audience the idea that a boy could find divinity in the equestrian image.

Topics for Further Study

- Compare and contrast the beliefs that Alan's mother and father have on concepts such as class, religion, sex, and, of course, horses. What effect have each of the parents had on Alan's development?

- Dora Strang describes the religious picture which hung above Alan's bed as "a little extreme" in its depiction of Christ "loaded down with chains," being beaten by Roman soldiers on his way to crucifixion. Research the figure of Christ in the history of Western art, analyzing some of the different ways in which he has been depicted. What do you think disturbed Alan about Jesus and the Christian religion as a whole? What prompted him to start his own religion?

- Discuss whether *Equus* ultimately seems to be supportive or critical of the value of psychoanalysis.

- Research the theories of Carl Jung, who Shaffer has called "one of the greatest minds of the twentieth century." Drawing on Jung's concept of archetypal images and other aspects of his philosophy, discuss the importance of the horse (and the centaur) as a symbol in *Equus*.

- Research the mythology and religious practice of Classical Greece. Discuss the significance of this pagan culture to the themes and characters of *Equus*. In particular, how does Shaffer's play enact the philosophical clash between the Apollonian, or rational, and the Dionysian, or instinctive?

- Research Sigmund Freud's theories of human psychology, including such concepts as Id/Ego/Superego, transference, repression, and defense mechanisms. Use as many of the concepts as seem applicable to provide a Freudian analysis of Alan's childhood development and how he came to commit his particular act of violence.

Memory and Reminiscence

A form of reminiscence—the replaying of scenes from the past—provides *Equus* with a dramatic structure. Memory, especially repressed memory that must be brought to light, is additionally an important thematic component in the play. In a classic Freudian formula, Alan has repressed certain memories in his subconscious and as a result suffers nightmares and other forms of mental unrest. Dr. Dysart uses techniques such as hypnosis and a "truth drug" placebo to lower Alan's psychic defenses and allow these repressed memories to rise to the surface, where they can be confronted and treated by the psychiatrist. There is an abreaction, a venting of psychic pain, which takes the form of theatrical performance and provides each act with an expressionistic conclusion (Alan on one of his midnight rides at the end of Act One; his recollection of blinding the horses near the end of Act Two).

Sanity and Insanity

Like the theme of religion, this theme operates on many levels in the play. Dysart is confronted, on the one hand, with a boy who is psychologically troubled, has committed a violent act society views as insane, and whose pain can be removed by treatment. The play unfolds dramatically, in fact, precisely because of Dysart's success in uncovering Alan's repressed memories, and it concludes with the implication that Dysart can cure Alan's distress. But in treating Alan, Dysart begins to view these labels of sanity and insanity as social constructions, values which appear fixed but actually change greatly over time and across cultures. Dysart is scared that by curing Alan, making the boy sane in a socially-accepted manner, he might take away from Alan a passion for life which most people never feel (and which Dysart admits he envies).

Sex

Sex and religion are probably the two most significant, and closely intertwined themes, in the play. Both are crucial factors in Alan's childhood development; in both instances, Alan makes a transference of what society views as "normal" forms of sex and worship onto his pagan, equine religion. The play hints at the sexual undertones of many events in Alan's childhood. Frank Strang's comment that Christianity to him "is just bad sex," and his reference to a particularly graphic depiction of Christ's crucifixion as "kinky," imply connections between sexual desire and religious ecstasy which the father may have instilled in Alan as a youth. Alan's ride with the Horseman is also given sexual undertones, a pleasure he is clearly attempting to replicate on his naked, midnight rides with Equus. (Alan has essentially made a religious practice out of a masturbatory act.) At the play's climax, Alan is confused when he finds himself sexually aroused by Jill Mason. He feels great shame as a result both of his "infidelity" in the presence of Equus and his inability to actually have intercourse with Jill. Sex is thus a major factor both in Alan's development, and in the violent act which initiates the dramatic action of the play.

Dramatic Genre

Equus closely resembles a suspense thriller in form and structure, revealing Shaffer's fondness for detective stories. Dysart is much like a classic sleuth solving a crime; he painstakingly tracks down the factors that led Alan to blind the six horses. Shaffer has worked in many dramatic genres, including domestic tragedy, farce, and historical drama. Many critics have noted that what makes *Equus* a unique theatrical experience is its seamless incorporation of several dramatic genres. In addition to being a serviceable suspense tale, the play has also been credited for its intriguing examination of the roots of mental illness as well as its canny updating of Greek tragedy. The play's popularity among audiences and critics has been attributed to its ability to appeal to numerous tastes. Likewise, not linked to any one dramatic school of thought, Shaffer has demonstrated his versatility with each new play.

Point of View

In *Equus*—as he has in other plays such as *Amadeus*—Shaffer uses the dramatic device of the *raisonneur,* a kind of "color commentator" who directly addresses the audience, providing details that assist the viewer in understanding the play's action. Thus, the point of view of *Equus* is largely that of Dysart (the play's *raisonneur*), who provides the context in which the story unfolds. However, certain elements in the play are clearly presented from Alan's perspective: the flashbacks are a theatrical reenactment of Alan's memories.

Staging

The set for *Equus,* rather than being realistic, is flexible and allows for numerous different performing spaces. The almost cinematic structure of the play—multiple, brief scenes in numerous locations—requires rapid changes in staging. This effect is achieved through a rotating turntable as well as other set techniques such as spot lighting and sparse use of props. For example, Alan picks up benches at one point and moves them, forming three stalls for a scene at Dalton's stables. The use of mimed objects and actions is also significant to the play's theatrical technique. Clive Barnes wrote in the *New York Times* that Shaffer "has his theatre set up here as a kind of bullring with a section of the audience actually sitting on stage." In addition to members of the audience, all the actors are seated on stage, rising to perform in scenes and then being seated, still in view of the audience. Thus, there is little separation between stage and audience, creating an intimacy which underscores the intensity of the drama. Irving Wardle wrote in the London *Times* that the stage "combines the elements of rodeo, stable, and Greek amphitheatre."

Temporal Organization

Rather than moving forward in strictly linear time, *Equus* combines a main plot unfolding in the present with repeated flashbacks to past events. Dysart's opening monologue in each act, and some of the therapy sessions with Alan, take place in the present. Incidents involving Alan's childhood and the night of his crime are in flashback, as are the sequences in Dysart's life that lead up to his treating the boy. The different temporal threads are woven together, with overlapping elements providing points of transition.

For example, the Nurse's comments to Dysart about Alan's condition are melded with Dysart later relating the same details to Hesther. By staging both events on stage at the same time, Shaffer achieves a kind of cinematic edit that allows the same topic to be simultaneously discussed in two distinct settings. The Nurse tells Dysart that Alan has been having nightmares during which he repeatedly screams "Ek!" Hesther, however, not Dysart, asks "Ek?" but the Nurse continues, "Yes, Doctor. Ek." The past is revealed in glimpses, usually an acting out of what one character is telling another in the present. As these memories are recalled in the present, lighting and set placement allow the actors to slip to another part of the stage and enact the past event being described.

Catharsis

Many critics have called *Equus* a "modern

tragedy," some evoking Aristotle's principles of tragedy (as he outlines in his *Poetics*) to discuss the manner in which the play operates. While *Equus* does not truly follow the formula for tragedy, it does contain many of the genre's important components. One of the most closely related is that of catharsis: the purgation of feelings of pity and fear, which Aristotle identified as the social function of tragedy. Parallel to the concept of catharsis is that of abreaction, the discharge of the emotional energy supposed to be attached to a repressed idea, especially by the conscious verbalization of that idea in the presence of a therapist. Thus, the staging of Alan's repressed memories has a therapeutic purpose that mirrors the potential cathartic effect of the play upon an audience.

Philosophical Content

The 1964 full-length play *Royal Hunt of the Sun: A Play Concerning the Conquest of Peru* introduced Shaffer's characteristic technique of opposing two central figures (in that play's case, the Inca king Atahualpa and the Spanish conquistador Francisco Pizarro) whose actions establish a dialectic on complex philosophical questions. This technique revealed itself again in the pairing of Dr. Dysart and Alan and would later resurface with the characters of Mozart and Salieri in Shaffer's 1979 play, *Amadeus*. Dysart and Alan stand, respectively, as philosophical representatives for subdued rationalism and passionate instinct. As the factors underlying Alan's violent act are revealed, Dysart discovers a dilemma of his own. Ridding Alan of his mental conflicts only succeeds in transferring them onto Dysart himself.

The Horse Chorus

In Greek theatre, the masked chorus serves to comment on the action of the play. Shaffer has a similar concept in mind with his chorus, although they make equine noises of humming, thumping, and stamping rather than speaking. In the early scenes concerning Alan's interaction with horses, the choral noises intensify the emotional content, making a connection between the early scenes and the foreshadowing of the act Alan will later commit. This non-realistic technique allows the audience a glimpse into Alan's state of mind—for the noise, as Shaffer comments, "heralds or illustrates the presence of Equus the God."

Among the chorus are six actors who represent Nugget and the other horses in the play. No attempt is made to make them appear realistic; they wear horse-like masks of wire and leather beneath which the heads of the actors are visible. Barnes observed that while "is not easy to present men playing horses on stage without provoking giggles . . . here the horses live up to their reputed godhead." Mollie Panter-Downes commented in the *New Yorker* that "these masked presences standing in the shadows of the stable manage to suggest the eeriness and power of. . . the old hoofed god."

When Alan mounts Nugget for the first time, all the other horses lean forward to create a visual picture that highlights Alan's belief that his god Equus resides in all horses. By having the same actor play the Horseman and Nugget, a visual connection is established which suggests Alan's transference of emotions from humans onto horses.

Historical Context

Equus premiered in 1973, near the beginning of a decade largely characterized in Britain by crisis and economic decline. Recovering from the ruins of World War II, Britain slowly built prosperity on a moderately socialist model. Many private institutions were nationalized, but the foreign debt tripled. The Labour government of the late-1960s lost ground due to the eroding economic situation, especially the monetary devaluation crisis of 1967, in which the country's currency dropped precipitously against other world markets.

Although the economy improved slightly in 1969, the Conservative Party rose to power in the election of 1970. Regarding foreign policy, the disastrous Suez Crisis of 1956, in which England lost control of the vital Suez Canal shipping passage, suggested strongly that Britain was no longer a major world power. Since the height of the British Empire in the early twentieth century, important possessions had been surrendered (most significantly, independence was granted to India, one of the Empire's colonial jewels, in 1947). Beginning in the late 1950s, the British government followed a deliberate policy of decolonization, one that systematically dismantled the country's once vast system of colonies.

In the early 1970s the British government continued to struggle with inflation. Violence plagued Northern Ireland, as battles between Protestant and Catholic factions continued to erupt. Both problems would dog British governments throughout the decade. In early 1974, Conservatives lost the general elections in the midst of a coal miners' strike. The government's refusal to capitulate to the miners' demands forced energy rationing and a fuel-conserving three-day work week. Although victorious, the Labour party lacked a full majority in Parliament, significantly limiting their power to enact policies in support of working people. Labour won a full majority of Parliamentary seats in October, 1974, but Britain continued to be plagued by inflation and economic decline. Widespread economic discontent led eventually to the victory of the Conservatives in 1979, and the election of Prime Minister Margaret Thatcher, whose term in office would be riddled with controversy, partisan battles, and wildly fluctuating public support.

Compare & Contrast

- **1973:** Children are widely viewed as innocent, and an act of violence like that committed by Alan is considered especially perplexing. As Hesther observes of Alan's actions in *Equus,* even psychiatric professionals "are going to be disgusted by the whole thing."

  Today: Rates of violent crime

committed by children have skyrocketed in the latter decades of the twentieth century. While the U.S. has been shocked by a rash adolescent violence—notably a series of shootings at schools in 1998—violent crimes by children are less a factor of life in Britain. Through isolated incidents and exposure to international media, however, British society has been made aware of the propensity for violence among troubled youth.

- **1973:** While the Conservative Party controls Parliament, the British Labour party is developing strength and will win important elections in the following year. After several more years of recession and other economic problems, however, voters will usher in a new Conservative government in 1979, led by Prime Minister Margaret Thatcher.

  Today: Ending eighteen years of Conservative Party control of the Parliament, the Labour Party achieves an overwhelming national election victory in 1997. Tony Blair becomes Prime Minister, but many feel that "New Labour" has abandoned so many of its traditionally leftist policies that the election is not so much a victory for working class people in Britain as it might appear.

- **1973:** Britain, like many nations in the industrialized West, is in the midst of an economic crisis characterized by wild inflation and labor unrest.

  Today: The economy has largely stabilized. Conservative governments held down inflation in the 1980s and early-1990s and privatized many national industries. The social cost of these policies, however, was a widening of the gap between rich and poor in Britain, cause for even more class resentment like that expressed by Frank Strang in *Equus*.

- **1973:** The British are a people known for their love of animals and are especially reverent toward horses. Shaffer must carefully tailor his depiction of Alan's crime so that *Equus* will startle audiences without sickening and outraging them. The 1977 film adaptation of the play depicts the blinding of the horses in a realistic and bloody fashion, drawing protests from animal-rights activists and criticism from Shaffer himself.

Today: The British, like every culture so heavily exposed to the media, have been forced to adjust to ubiquitous images of violence. The welfare of animals, however, continues to be of great concern in Britain, where animals-rights activism is much more common than in other countries.

On October 6, 1973, Egypt and Syria attacked Israel, both sides blaming the other for having initiated the new aggression (Israel had shot down two Syrian jets). The Yom Kippur War (named for the Jewish Holy Day of Atonement on which the conflict began) was the fourth Arab-Israeli war since 1948. The Soviet union gave military support to the Arabs in response to U.S. support of Israel. Thus, the war had a distinctly Cold War context in which Britain was also implicated.

The greatest impact of the Arab-Israeli war on the West, however, was the resulting oil embargo by Arab members of the Organization of Petroleum Exporting Countries (OPEC). The oil embargo exacerbated an energy crisis that was already gripping the world. Connected to the energy crisis and other factors, the West additionally experienced an inflation crisis; annual double-digit inflation became a reality for the first time for most industrial nations. The oil shock and soaring grain prices precipitated a world monetary crisis and then a worldwide economic recession, the worst since the Great Depression of the 1930s. In Britain, these economic contractions contributed to an increasing sense of social hopelessness.

The Bahamas gained full independence July 10, 1973, after 256 years as a British crown colony. The British Empire continued its inexorable progress toward decolonization. As British control was waning in far-flung parts of the world they once dominated, so British independence was challenged by the growing movement toward union among Western European nations. In 1973, Britain joined the European Community after a decade of controversy, agreeing to participate in common decisions on trade, agriculture, industry, the environment, foreign policy, and defense. In 1993, the European Union (E.U.) was created following ratification of the Maastricht Treaty. Britain is today an uneasy member of the E.U.; they would not take part, for example, in the creation of a common currency, the euro, which debuted on world markets on January 4, 1999.

Across the Atlantic, 1973 was also a tumultuous year in American society. American troops were withdrawn from the war in Vietnam but bombing raids on that country continued. The U.S. launched *Sky lab,* its first space station. The U.S. Supreme Court legalized abortion in their landmark decision *Roe* v. *Wade.* Public approval for President Richard Nixon continued to plummet, as accusations and evidence continued to support the fact that he had granted approval for the June 17,

1972, burglary of Democratic National Committee offices at the Watergate complex in Washington. Like public opinion over Vietnam, Watergate was an important symbol both of stark divisions in American society and a growing disillusionment with the integrity of national leaders. In late 1973, Vice President Spiro Agnew resigned under pressure, pleading no contest (*no lo contendre*) to charges of income tax evasion and consequently setting the tone for scandals that would continue to rock the executive branch (Nixon himself, under threat of impeachment and removal from office, resigned the following year; other cabinet members, such as Nixon's Attorney General, John Mitchell, and Chief of Staff, H. R. Haldeman, would also be implicated in the crime).

Culturally, London had in the 1960s become a world capital of theatre, fashion, and popular music, but this image was tarnished somewhat by ongoing the economic decline. Save some notable exceptions, 1973 was not a banner year for the London theatre: Alan *Ayckbourn's Absurd Person Singular* and David Storey's *Cromwell* being two of the few works to share acclaim with Shaffer's *Equus*. On the American stage, 1973 saw the premier of Lanford Wilson's *Hot I Baltimore,* Neil Simon's *The Good Doctor,* and the blockbuster musical *A Little Night Music* by Stephen Sondheim.

Critical Overview

When *Equus* premiered on July 26, 1973, it provoked strong reactions from critics, as might be expected given the play's startling topic and innovative production. Many reviews praised the philosophical and theatrical complexity of the work, heralding it as the high point of Shaffer's dramatic career. Dissenting reviews called the play pretentious or contrived; few writers, however, failed to observe that the play was a major theatrical event of the 1973 London season. Michael Billington of the Manchester *Guardian* described the play as "sensationally good." Billington observed that Shaffer continued to explore a theme common to his earlier works but judged *Equus* superior to its predecessors because in it, "the intellectual argument and the poetic imagery are virtually indivisible." Harold Hobson of the *Sunday Times* similarly raved about the play.

Taking an opposing view, Ian Christie of the *Daily Express* called the script "pretentious, philosophical claptrap." Irving Wardle of the daily London *Times,* meanwhile, was among the critics who expressed a mixed opinion. Wardle thought some of Dysart's speeches were excellently written and found the central image of the horse "poetically inexhaustible," but he found much of Shaffer's writing contrived. "There is very little real dialogue," Wardle wrote. "Even the interviews consist of solo turns introduced with wary parleys on both sides." Wardle faulted Shaffer's dramatic creations as heavy handed, calling his characters "schematic automaton[s]."

While many critics, even those who appreciate Shaffer's work, have pointed out the many similarities between his plays (Wardle called *Equus* a "variation on a theme"), Clive Barnes saluted the originality of this play. *Equus,* he wrote in the *New York Times,* "is quite different from anything Mr. Shaffer has written before, and has, to my mind, a quite new sense of seriousness to it." Although still intended as a popular play, *Equus* "has a most refreshing and mind-opening intellectualism." Writing about the New York production (which opened October 24, 1974), Barnes commented that *Equus* "adds immeasurably to the fresh hopes we have for Broadway's future." Walter Kerr, in another *New York Times* review, similarly found Shaffer's play to be of great stature. "*Equus,*" he wrote, "is one of the most remarkable examples of stagecraft, as well as of sustained and multifaceted sensibility, the contemporary theatre has given us." Building on such acclaim, the Broadway production of *Equus* enjoyed an exceptionally long run of 1209 performances.

Initial criticism of *Equus* focused on such questions as whether the intellectual content of the play melded well with its dramatic form and content and whether or not Peter Shaffer's dialogue was up to par with the play's theatrical production, which was widely viewed as ingenious. In more extended analyses of the work, critics began to delve deeply into the psychological complexity of *Equus,* drawing out a number of interrelated themes. As intellectual touchstones, critics have elucidated elements of *Equus* by referring to the work of Sigmund Freud and Carl Jung as well as the philosopher Friedrich Nietzsche. Articles have variously drawn upon Freud's theories of childhood development and the human subconscious, Jung's philosophies of archetypal images, and Nietzsche's concept of tragedy (based upon the human failure to transcend individuation).

Starting with Freudian principles, critics have analyzed the structure of the play as a therapeutic reenactment, or abreaction, of memories repressed in Alan's subconscious. Many articles have illustrated how the play functions primarily as a study of human sexual development. "Here," wrote John Weightman in *Encounter,* "was a new and interesting example of the way sex can get mixed up with religion, or *vice versa.*"

Additionally, many critics have focused on the play's religious themes independent of their relationship with sexual development. In such an analysis, Alan is a product of conflicting religious impulses, one Christian, one pagan. More broadly, many critics see an ongoing process of theological introspection as a fundamental element of Shaffer's drama. James R. Stacy, in *Peter Shaffer: A Casebook,* observed that Shaffer has been engaged on a "search for worship." John M. Clum, meanwhile, commented in the *South Atlantic Quarterly* that Shaffer has been "fascinated with the impulse toward faith. For him the adversary of the man of faith is not a cosmic void or universal chaos; it is rationality. . . . Shaffer is not concerned with existence of a god: he is fascinated with man's need for religion, for transcendence, for passionate submission."

Wardle, J. W. Lambert, Frank Lawrence, and Doyle W. Walls are among critics who have evoked the cultural associations with the Greek gods Apollo and Dionysus as a way of contextualizing the play's intellectual conflict between subdued rationalism (widely viewed as normality) and passionate instinct (viewed as insanity). Lambert wrote in *Drama* that in this, *Equus* focuses on "a theme constant throughout human history, never resolved, always relevant, and very much in the air today."

Equus continues to attract critical inquiry because of its psychological complexity, its theatrical innovation, and its enduring philosophical weight. Writing in *Peter Shaffer: A Casebook,* Dennis Klein marveled that Shaffer "has so carefully constructed it that there are no loose ends left for the audience to tie together; and yet the play has inspired such diverse interpretations." Recent critics, reviewing more than four active decades of writing by Shaffer, still consider the success of *Equus* an important benchmark in the playwright's artistic development. C. J. Gianakaris wrote in *Peter Shaffer* that *"Five Finger Exercise* and *The Royal Hunt of the Sun* signaled the arrival on the scene of a new, innovative voice in the theatre; *Equus* confirmed it."

What Do I Read Next?

- *Amadeus,* often regarded as Shaffer's greatest dramatic achievement. The 1979 play is a probing exploration of the human psyche, centering on the court composer Antonio Salieri and his jealousy for fellow composer Wolfgang Amadeus Mozart, who is portrayed as a vulgar, self-centered musical genius. The play won the 1980 Antoinette (Tony) Perry Award. In 1984, the film adaptation won Academy Awards for best picture and best screenplay adaptation, which Shaffer composed from his original text.

- *The Royal Hunt of the Sun,* a 1964 play which secured Shaffer's reputation as an accomplished dramatist. The play—which creatively blends ritual, dance, music, and drama—reenacts the sixteenth-century Spanish conquest of the Incan empire. Like *Equus* and *Amadeus,* this play employs two opposing central characters to create not only dramatic tension but also a philosophical dialectic on central themes.

- *One Flew over the Cuckoo's Nest,* by Ken Kesey (Viking, 1962). Set in a mental institution and told through from the perspective of Chief Bromden, a Native American patient, Kesey's book was adapted for the stage and made into one of the most successful films of all time. The novel depicts the struggle between the wild and free-spirited Randal McMurphy and the autocratic Nurse Ratched, offering an unqualified criticism of the treatment of individuals at the hands of the psychiatric institution.

- *The Butcher Boy,* by Patrick McCabe (Fromm, 1993). This novel (recently adapted into a film by Neil Jordan) explores the descent into madness of a boy who has experienced a harsh upbringing in a small Irish town. Like Alan in *Equus,* Francie Brady inhabits a world largely of his own imagination. Francie's growing antagonism toward the society around him culminates with an act of startling violence.

- *The Myth of Mental Illness: Foundations of a Theory of Personal Conduct* by Thomas Szasz, M.D. (revised edition, Harper Row, 1974). Szasz is the author of dozens of iconoclastic books challenging the fundamental principles of the psychiatric industry. In this ground breaking work, he argues that human behavior has reasons rather than causes, dissects what he views as flaws in the medical model of mental illness, and challenges the notion of psychiatrists as beneficent healers.

Sources

Barnes, Clive. *"Equus* a New Success on Broadway"* in the *New York Times,* October 25, 1974, p. 26.

Billington, Michael. Review of *Equus* in the Manchester *Guardian,* July 27, 1973, p. 12.

Christie, Ian. Review of *Equus* in the *Daily Express* (London), July 27, 1973, p. 10.

Clum, John M. "Religion and Five Contemporary Plays: The Quest for God in a Godless World" in the *South Atlantic Quarterly,* Vol. 77, no. 4, 1978, pp. 418-32.

Hewes, Henry. "The Crime of Dispassion" in the *Saturday Review,* January 25, 1975, p. 54.

Hughes, Catherine. "London's Stars Come Out" in *America,* December 8, 1973, pp. 443-44.

Kerr, Walter. *"Equus:* A Play That Takes Risks and Emerges Victorious" in the *New York Times,* November 3, 1974, p. 11.

Klein, Dennis A. "Game-Playing in Four Plays by Peter Shaffer" in *Peter Shaffer: A Casebook,* edited by C. J. Gianakaris, Garland (New York), 1991, pp. 95-113.

Lambert, J. W. Review of *Equus* in *Drama* (London), Vol. III, 1973, pp.14-16.

Lawrence, Frank. "The *Equus* Aesthetic: The

Doctor's Dilemma" in *Four Quarters,* Vol. 29, no. 2, 1980, pp. 13-18.

Panter-Downes, Mollie. "Letter from London" in the *New Yorker,* November 12, 1973, pp. 181-84.

Peter Shaffer ("English Authors Series," Vol. 261, revised edition), Twayne, 1993.

Shaffer, Peter. *"Equus:* Playwright Peter Shaffer Interprets Its Ritual" in *Vogue,* February, 1975, p. 136.

Stacy, James R. "The Sun and the Horse: Peter Shaffer's Search for Worship" in *Peter Shaffer: A Casebook,* edited by C. J. Gianakaris, Garland, 1991, pp. 95-113.

Walls, Doyle W. *"Equus:* Shaffer, Nietzsche, and the Neuroses of Health" in *Modern Drama,* Vol. 27, no. 3, 1984, pp. 314-23.

Wardle, Irving. "Shaffer's Variation on a Theme" in the *Times* (London), July 27, 1973, p. 15.

Weightman, John. "Christ As Man and Horse" in *Encounter,* Vol. 44, no. 3, 1975, pp. 44-46.

Further Reading

Contemporary Literary Criticism, Gale: Volume 5, Volume 14, Volume 18, Volume 37, Volume 60.

> This resource compiles selections of criticism; it is an excellent starting point for a research paper about Shaffer. The selections in these five volumes span Shaffer's career. For an overview of Shaffer's life, see the entry on him in Volume 13 of the *Dictionary of Literary Biography.* Also see Volume 7 of Gale's *Drama Criticism.*

Cooke, Virginia, and Malcom Page, compilers. *File on Shaffer,* Methuen, 1987.

> This slim but excellent resource reprints excerpts from a wide variety of sources (reviews, interviews, etc.). It also includes a chronology of works, production, and publication data as well as information on Shaffer's non-theatrical works.

Eberle, Thomas. *Peter Shaffer: An Annotated Bibliography,* Garland, 1991.

> A resource intended to serve the needs of both teachers/students of dramatic literature and theatre professionals. Organized with each

major play as a separate chapter. The bibliographic entries are subdivided as follows: editions of the text, play reviews, news reports and feature stories, scholarly essays, and (where applicable) film adaptations and reviews. The span of this work is from March, 1956, to May, 1990 (through *Lettice and Lovage*). It also contains a complete chronology of Shaffer's plays and additional chapters covering general works (biographies and works analyzing more than one play), interviews, and Shaffer's early works (prior to *Five Finger Exercise*).

"*EQUUS* EMERGES AS A SURPRISINGLY PAINLESS MODERN TRAGEDY, WHICH ACCOUNTS FOR BOTH ITS POPULARITY AND THE RESERVATIONS SOME SERIOUS CRITICS HAVE EXPRESSED ABOUT ITS SIGNIFICANCE"

Gianakaris, C. J. *Peter Shaffer,* Macmillan (New York), 1992.

A book-length study of Shaffer and his works. Gianakaris writes of Shaffer, "*Five Finger Exercise* and *The Royal Hunt of the Sun* signaled the arrival on the scene of a new, innovative voice in the theatre;

Equus confirmed it." In his analysis of specific plays, Gianakaris defines the common threads of theme and technique which run through many of Shaffer's theatrical works.

Gianakaris, C. J., editor. *Peter Shaffer: A Casebook* ("Casebook on Modern Dramatists" series, Vol. 10), Garland, 1991.

This collection includes ten essays on Shaffer and a 1990 interview with the playwright. Many of the selections offer comparative readings of Shaffer's major works. Also included are a comprehensive index of opening dates for Shaffer's plays and an abbreviated bibliography.

Klein, Dennis A. *Peter Shaffer,* revised edition, Twayne, 1993.

A general study of Shaffer's works by a critic who has also published on *Equus* in particular ("Peter Shaffer's *Equus* as a Modern Aristotelian Tragedy" in *Studies in Iconography,* Vol. 9, 1983). The opening section provides an outline of Shaffer's life and discusses his early and minor works. Each chapter on one of the major plays provides sections on the plot; the major characters; sources, symbols, and themes; structure and stagecraft; and critical appraisal.

Lightning Source UK Ltd.
Milton Keynes UK
UKHW021120230821
389329UK00015B/1267

9 781375 379557